Kintsugi

poems by

Kate Leboff

Finishing Line Press
Georgetown, Kentucky

Kintsugi

Copyright © 2024 by Kate Leboff
ISBN 979-8-88838-606-4 First Edition
All rights reserved under International and Pan-American Copyright Conventions. No part of this book may be reproduced in any manner whatsoever without written permission from the publisher, except in the case of brief quotations embodied in critical articles and reviews.

Publisher: Leah Huete de Maines
Editor: Christen Kincaid
Cover Art: Adobe Stock images by Leart and YouandIgraphics
Author Photo: Scott Levine
Cover Design: Kate Leboff

Order online: www.finishinglinepress.com
also available on amazon.com

Author inquiries and mail orders:
Finishing Line Press
PO Box 1626
Georgetown, Kentucky 40324
USA

Contents

Dedication ix
Note from the Author xi
"Sweet Pea 1
ni mi voz bajaré 4
Pitch 6
You confuse overdramatic 7
When I cannot sleep, neurons pinging 9
inner child reawakening 10
A storm cloud of starlings 12
I watch 14
Om(i)en(ous) 16
Secret swim spot 18
Wildflowers 20
"A smart man learns from his own mistakes . . ." 22
The Aftermath 24
The Fear 26
(Un)Becoming Carolyn 28
Wild Thing 40
Coming out of the closet 43
The world might be a little better 45
The barefoot stubbed toe in the dark 47
for the first time 49
Self-inflicted story/lines 50
Gutted 52
Kintsugi 54
Foggy 64
Drowning 65
Rush hour 67

Epitomized	68
Unaccountable	70
I wonder	74
I was sturdy	76
Narcotize	79
Misogynists take note	81
Betrayal	82
Any(but) w(here)	84
To all the fish in the sea	85
Limitless Interrogatives	87
my mind begs the question	88
"Oh lawd"	90
Punctuate	93
Unwelcome return	94
Disassociating	96
Deactivated	98
Cheers	99
Malaise	101
Unmotivation	102
Bird Dog Whiskey	103
Too little, too late	104
I am folded	105
Fool's gold	107
Antidote	108
you took me swimming	110
Upstate Mid-September	113
Requited	114
you're somethin' else	115
I love you	117
Grounded	119
Wordless Chorus	121

Written/in-between	122
"I ain't. We will."	124
You called	126
Dreamt of you	127
say(ing) what you (don't) mean	128
Addendum to Antidote	129
> We ain't friends?	132
Di(e)spa(i)rity	133
I walk home	135
Lonely Sound	137
Unhaunted	139
Play with at your own risk	141
Rabbit Run Rd.	144

*For my mother and father;
my sister, sister-in-law, and brothers;*

my paternal grandmother, Carolyn;

my heart dog and soulmate, Luna;

and my high school English teacher, Mrs. Rogers.

Note from the Author

Dearest reader,

This collection deserves a trigger warning, whether you know me or not. And if you do know me, and perhaps even call me friend or family, this was essential.

I hope you will remember these are just a handful of instances in a full life. A life that has held so many more moments of love, happiness, laughter, enthusiasm, and support. I am blessed with and grateful for a wonderful family, an amazing group of friends, an unparalleled community, and the unconditional love of my two dogs. The poems included here are fleeting moments in my life recorded over the past fifteen years and thoroughly edited in the past year and a half.

Though, many of the events and much of the trauma were not so fleeting, unfortunately.

There are also poems of joyous and beautiful moments.

However, I should note that a majority of this book mentions or contains instances of self-harm; sexual assault; mental illness; drug and alcohol abuse; domestic violence; mental, emotional, and physical abuse; suicide and suicide ideation; and death.

Despite this, I hope you read on. This book is meant, as a whole, to be a hand to hold when things seem hopeless. When you feel as if there is no one in this world who could understand. When the light of day never seems to come to chase away the shadows of the night. When you feel death whispering in your ear.... I hope this books finds you.

Kintsugi, after all, is an art that resonates with hope and healing. Rebuilding and reinventing oneself. We sometimes must break to create a masterpiece.

It does get better. Keep going.

I am so glad that I did. As are so many others. I know you can too.

—Kate

"Sweet Pea"

Her father (im)planted
with the seed of their daughter
his wife's / her mother's
womb—twenty years young but ready—
as inter/entwined lovers,
clinging to one another
as do the climbing vines of helix hedera.

The first sonogram seemed to bear
the XY sex. A boy's name
chosen: Zachary Hunter.
But the germinating embryo
was unexpectedly YY chromosomed
and delivered a small daughter,
"Peanut," her father called her.

Her mother and father cultivated
and watered their "Sweet Pea"
as flourishing gardeners
having just birthed their first child
—a son, "Bubba"—the year
prior and they tended (to be)
loving(ly) to her constant colicky cries
despite sleepless night after night.

Her mother's and father's lathyrus odoratus
from sprout to seedling
to budding to flowering into wildly
vividly solidly thriving blooming
bicolored, streaked, and flaked
brilliant blues, vibrant violets, pastel pinks,
indigos, purest whites.

Their "Sweet Pea" now at the stage
to decide her nutrients, maintain
her own growth, reproduce if she chooses
(but won't), express the shades, tints, hues
sui generis to her and those she most embraces.

Unique from their four other sown flora,
but equally as admired and adored,
an Autumn Joy vased
in a centerpieced place
season to season, year to year.

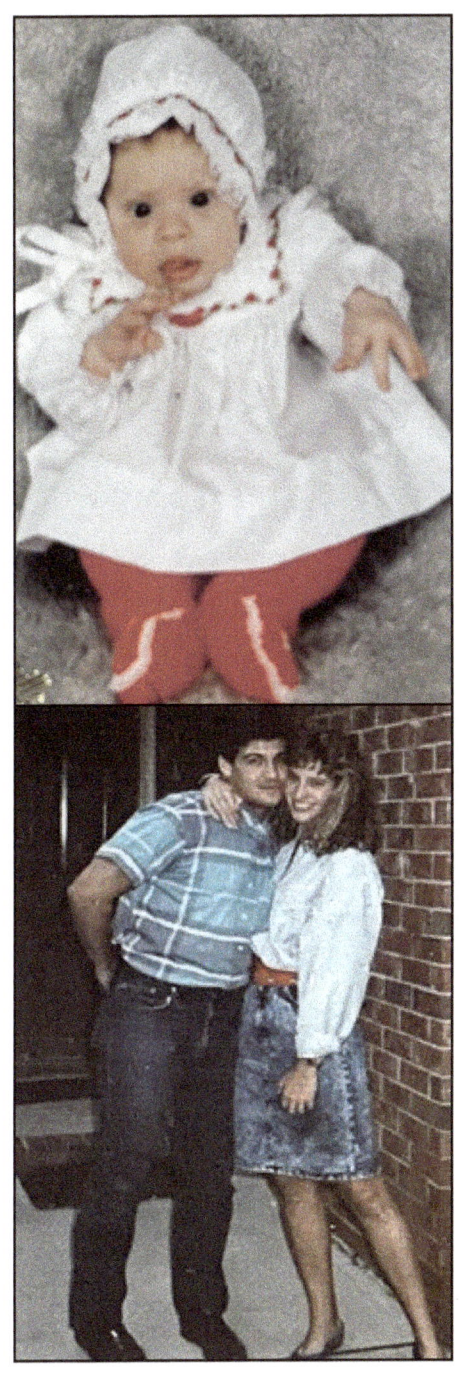

ni mi voz bajaré

"You
just have a very loud voice…"

You just have a very loud voice

You just have a VERY loud voice

[I]

*just have
a very*

L O U D

voice.

*Yo podría /
[quizás] debería
ser / haber sido*

más alta.

I shall remain
orgullosa y salvaje.

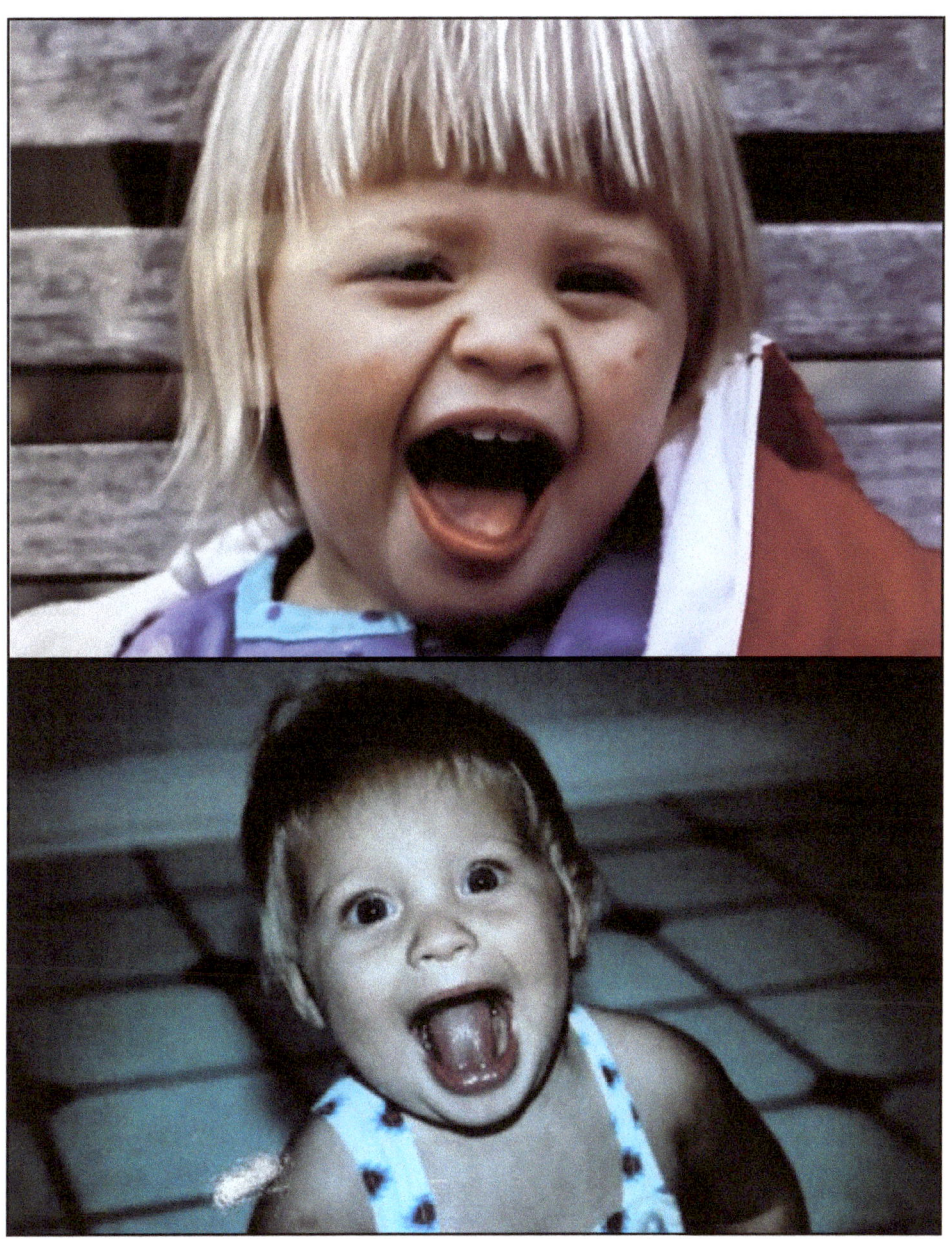

Pitch

I am waiting for words
to excavate the marrow
and tw(i)ang(e) tendons,
fiddling out, bow
on strings, a quickened
pace. I am waiting
to strike the chords
of my voice.

I am waiting,
in the static,
a quaking
noise.

You confuse overdramatic

with passion
and sincerity
unfiltered feeling
felt unfilteredly.
Considered weighted words
waitedly but delivered naturally
and unapologetically.

Being great, said Emerson,
*is being
misunderstood.*

Being insane is sanity
according to
Bukowski.

Being an open book misread
by the majority of those I encounter;
being the character others (I) cannot (can) seem to close read.

I am grateful for each layer
of person worn and shed
and glad each time I am
again more soft-bellied.

When I cannot sleep, neurons pinging

words and sentences stringing
a cacophony
chaotically musically
along cranial synapses
inso/maniacally
manically
bipolarly
panicky,

I write
skin to pen to paper
black-inked loops and lines.

Writing does not aid in sleep,

but, at least,

I am being productive.

inner child reawakening

This is a reawakening

or perhaps a rekindling
of a flickering, waning flame.

I am blazing once more

like the young girl at six
running over rocks, snapping sticks
barefoot on callused soles and shirtless,
through the forest.

Howling at the sky, calling for her wolf kin.
An animal fur atop her small white-blonde head
and wielding a thin branch sharpened
by a Swiss Army knife.

At thirty-one, I am six again.
A crackling wildfire. A firecracker.

A storm cloud of starlings,

like plagued locusts,
eat up the gouached corals
and violently violets of the sunset sky
streaked with cotton candied cirrus
overhead, and no one
notices but the girl
with her head in the clouds.

Mountains with bowed backs,
night capped with snow,
rise up in haughty defiance;
no greenery to show, just white faces
blinding, and no one
notices but the girl,
whose soles/soul never touch/es the ground.

Titmice on a static staccatoed line
warm their feet;
a thousand tiny cheep cheeps
nip the air bites with frosted teeth
at their tail feathers,

and no one
notices but the girl.

I watch

as a hawk, red tail
staining the sky, *s h i f t s* the air
as she dives. Her prey
is found: a blur of brownish-grey
pumps his wings *a w a y*
from the reaper,

but natural selection
granted the hawk agility
and quickness: a hunter. This
sparrow or wren exists
to pluck noxious insects
from gardens, perfect
his songs,

but now dies
to subside
the gnaw of hunger
from the belly of a stronger
species.

The quarry
is caught; a *f l u r r y*
of earth-toned tufts
catch on a zephyr and gust
like dandelion seeds
on the breeze
of a child's wish.

Om(i)en(ous)

Is it good when a murder(-) of (-ous) crows
—carrying mouthfuls of carrion—perch upon
the eaves of the neighboring home
making and holding black-beaded eye
contact with anthropoid anole green
eyes as the caw(ll)ing black feathered species feasts?

An Edgar Allen Poe ome(i)n(ousness)
flying and (ar)resting with the rising
sun begging the crow-locked eyes of
a human's mind to consider:

Am I the writer of this foreboding in(por)tent(sion)?

Or am I the prot*(ant?)agonist* of an unseen novel*(sad)ist*?

Skeletal *(egregious?)* bones in your closet?
A sign (for *you*) to fear.

Snatched, collaterally damaged
skeletons in *another*'s?
Theirs to dread.
A fearsome sign to seek and exact revenge (?)

Secret swim spot

Where no one knows,
I sit sipping Sheldrake rosé,
pale toes ending in unpainted nails
in the cold Taughannock Creek.

I am watching crawfish scuttle and scoot by.
I notice, for the first time,
the way in which the sun strikes
the bubbled oxygen just below the surface
and showers tiny bursts of light
on the greenish blue-grey slate & shale shallowly
below, like faraway stars pinpricking
a wish upon night sky.

Wildflowers

I was waiting
in a blue hospital gown,
on a sterile white-linened cot.
I was waiting for
clarity, for release
from sterility, whiteness, frigidity,
fragility.
I was waiting for someone
to blame, to strike, to run to;

none came.

I was waiting
for him—
Cincinnati Reds baseball
cap, worn and faded,
subduing black-inked hair.
I was losing
hope; I was slipping
away,

when I heard:

Let's go home.
He held out his hand,
waiting.

The clouds passed;
I was planted,
watered, and began

waiting for
myself to (re)surface—
raw, bare, sober
yet still untamed
but drained of poison,
no longer a weed.

I am waiting for

the freedom
of wildflowers
but the discipline
to grow.

I am waiting for change,
and for much of the same
like Summer, Winter, Autumn,
Spring.

> "A smart man learns from his own mistakes.
> A wise man learns from the mistakes of others."

My father's loose repetition
of the adage

I disliked immediately,
from any person's mouth, but heard
most often from his lips.
My dislike for the expression
bloomed as a (the wild) child—
unsure then of why—

grew (in)to (black sheep) adolescence
then (anomalous) adulthood.

My father repeated the words
to my older brother and me
in our teenage and young adult years.

At the chair-scraping-the-floor
din of those seventeen words,
my nose would crinkle as if smelling ammonia.
My left eyebrow would arch like the spine
of a claws-out and hissing cat.
My anole green eyes would roll, but I bit
my tongue until I made the decision
to "say what I mean
and do what I say" at twenty-five.

At thirty-one, I am more than a little
banged up, bruised, bloodied, burnt,
mud-smattered, smeared, shattered,
but with no trepidation
of failure or pain or judgment.

My greatest fear:

missing out,
regretting the chances

I did not take,

not the mistakes
I have made (will) (make).

As the last breath
rattles from my body, I will
smile and say,
"I was a smart woman who
learnt from her own mistakes."

The Aftermath

Umbrella-like seeds not
plucked gently
by index and middle fingers
double crossed
hoping
"he loves me,"
against
he loves me
not.

Not on the warm breath
of a child's wish
against its head, drifting
on a gentle wind.

No warning
but the sudden rumbling
wind whistling
rasping of the trees
and the spindly fingers of light
across a crying sky.

Each floret blown away,
and only naked, vulnerable
stalks remain.

The dandelion, lion's tooth,
taraxacum officinale
still rooted
still standing
up to a sky
that could

not

tear her down.

The Fear

A walk alone in the twilit
night. The naked trees
gape and glare at bare feet
and a sparsely clothed body.
The fear of the unseen
greater than the shadowed silhouette,
on her left, with bared teeth.

The   s n a p   of twigs
and *s h i v e r* of ghostly wind
among the living and dead flora of the forest floor
bring her to feeble knees,

staring into the yellow eyes
of a wolf salivating.

His mouth beckons.
His breath warms the
chapped, frostbitten
skin of her cheeks and nose.
The wood echoes
with silence and cold.

The darkness of his jaws swallows

her and she welcomes it
and slides down his gullet,
knowing what she'll find.

(Un)Becoming Carolyn

I am (un)becoming (of) my grandmother.
Her willowy, lissome, lithe body
perched upon a splintering, wooden porch swing.
Double fisting a Virginia Slim—
filter stained by Elizabeth Arden-lipstick—a Sweet 'n Low
sugared and Creamora coffee embraced by slender fingers;
talons glossed in Revlon Raven Red.
She in a plaid flannel robe cast over a nightgown of faux scarlet silk;
pedicured toes pinched in sized ten, thrift store slippers.
Her thick, sable hair and sun-gilded skin
—indicative of her Cherokee ancestry—
in a bobbed bouffant with hints of White Diamonds cologne.
Gracile, long legs crossed
one over the other.

In stature, I stand five inches diminished,
swaybacked, and stocky on the patio of my parents' home.
The oversized graphic t-shirt
I did not return to my ex-partner
and my father's / her son's vintage, checkered jacket
hang past stout, muscled trunks of thigh and down to scarred knees.
My flat soled and calloused, sized eight feet
and underclad buttocks bare to the late lingering,
winter-chilled Virginia breeze carrying flakes of March snow.
Tattooed, hyperhidrosis-laden hands
ending in unadorned, anxiety-bitten fingernails.
Purplish baggage beneath exhausted anole green eyes;
a body traced with Native American blood pigmented
by the first weeks of Spring sun.
A lion's mane of waist length, honey blonde tresses
streaked with remnants of Manic Panic teal hair dye
and unscented except for tinges of nicotine and tobacco
and the off-brand shampoo of yesterday's shower.

An American Spirit
clenched between unpainted, chapped lips.
Fired from my job. Castaway by my first true love.
Marooned and broke(n) in the makeshift, unfinished basement
bachelorette pad in which I freeload as the vagrant,

stereotypical millennial in the home of my parents,
offering to pay rent with my unemployment checks
and gobbling up my parents' wifi
interrupting the internet connection
as I apply to hundreds of jobs daily.

A disoriented(at) twenty-five-year-old who has only given
my parents a grandchild in
the form of an equally
displaced and traumatized
rescue dog
prescribed the same Xanax dosage as I.

Hidden bottles of champagne, marijuana edibles,
and cigarettes consumed in (un)confidence—
"you're killing yourself with those cancer sticks,"
people say, unaware I revel in this idea of 'legal suicide.'
Drugs and toxins ingested to forget
for an hour, a few minutes, a singular moment.

I lost nineteen pounds of bodily
weight in less than fourteen days
from lack of sleep, lack of appetite, lack of ability—
under the strain—to keep the nauseating anxiety
at bay. This anatomical, animistic, cognizant
vessel and mentally ill brain
conspiring against me.

I betted the twelve dollars to my name
on a horse at Ponies & Pints
in downtown Richmond. The one night
I endeavored to enjoy an evening pretending
not to be in the situation I am in.
Pretending I have quit
bumming smokes, pretending I can pay for my own
drinks, pretending this life is not mine.
Pretending I am fine as my brother and his friends
end the night winning more than 1,200 dollars between them.
Maybe, it is time I take
my horse out of the race.

Hungover the next day,
eating ribs at Mission BBQ,
I discover my losing #2 pony's name:
"Given Up on Dreaming."
My older brother and I laugh
until I cry.

On my left wrist, a sprawl of helixed hedera—
almost concealing thick, white, kitchen knife-carved cicatrices—
a needle-inked memorial to my undiagnosed depression-riddled
grandmother stolen by breast cancer
and to her husband, a WWII German immigrant
misappropriated by the Vietnam War.

His ChapStick—applied from time to time: " a kiss from Johnny"—
and Army dog tags etched 27th Wolfhound Infantry
with his name, social security number, blood type, and religious preference
returned with nonexistent remains, two Purple Hearts,
two Bronze Star Medals, and a folded star-spangled flag.
Carolyn and Johnny, in life and love, always "clinging
to one another like ivy."

Carolyn, born in 1943, an independent, individualistic
firecracker her teenage years on—perhaps the moment she exited
Great Grandma Adelaide's womb.
Bold and vibrant as the costume jewelry she donned
and the shades of red painted on her nails and lips.
Made a widowed wife and single mother at twenty-four, my father aged six
and his brother just three. Men tried to date her.
She was the spitting image of Elizabeth Taylor.

Once a car salesman refused to move his Cadillac
intentionally parked behind her bright orange 1968 Mercury Cougar.
He would not cede until she agreed to go out with him.
When the man refused to remove his convertible, she "pulled a Carolyn:"
switched gears to reverse, hit the gas, and backed her fiery
coupe to force his out of the way.
"I'm going to get fired!" he screamed.
She tossed back "here's to hoping!"
and her young sons in the backseat tossing
their heads back laughing, jet black locks

blowing in the window-rolled-down wind.

During her second marriage,
she put a .38 Special to the forehead
of her abusive (eventual) ex-husband, threatening
"If you ever lay hands on my children again,
I'll blow your brains out." He never did.

When she was lost / when I lost her,
I was fourteen on the cusp of adolescence.
I would soon hit puberty, a late bloomer.
Mother Nature granting / cursing me with menstruation, hormonal changes.
Grandma Carolyn and I could talk until our mouths ran dry;
we could sit in quiet, honeyed harmony.
She introduced me to Charlie Pride, Jerry Lee Lewis, Fats Domino,
horror movies and Westerns, Waffle House,
how to dress and carry yourself as if you were
not impoverished, midnight madness sales, *Gone with the Wind*,
and that women are never "too pretty to talk / act like that."

She was sixty-three years young in hospice at my Uncle GJ's home.
A mere skeletal encasement for a wisp thin ghost of her spirit.
Her body remained, but her essence had long departed.
Her lizard green irises and yellow-rimmed pupils—
American Indian characteristics twins with mine—were vacant.
She took her final breaths
as my father / her son begged
I come and see her. I refused, never regretting this decision.

At twenty-five, I ousted Steve,
my cocaine dealing/addicted, alcoholic, child-abused boyfriend.
I once allowed him to nearly choke me to death, reasoning at the time
it might help him heal. Three months later, he was arrested for pummeling
the socket of my right eye. I could not hide the nightshade blue bruise and I did
not try.
The first and last time he assaulted my dog, Luna,
I broke his nose gushing blood, Luna cornered him snarling
in the bathroom, and I kicked him out of my home.

At thirty, I evicted my (soon to be) ex-husband, Chris,
a best friend of more than eight years. He metamorphosed into Mr. Hyde

two days post-marriage. A man on the verge of committing
some lasting physical damage,
having already left me with PTSD,
mental scarring, and one small scar
on my left shoulder from a steel troffer
thrown in a rage fit.
His undiagnosed intermittent explosiveness
and borderline personality disorder.
A cached cocktail of scripts
consumed spasmodically—
Klonopin, Viagra, Prozac, Adderall, Xanax—
chased round-the-clock by chewing tobacco, nicotine,
weed, and a double Old Fashioned
disguised in a to-go coffee mug.

Bound legally by a governmental piece of paper; separated
by a Remington shotgun barrel,
the bared teeth of two pitbulls,
552 miles, and an order of protection.

Two of the many occurrences Grandma Carolyn
spoke to / came to me / came to mind (?):
I stood on the top floor of a parking garage
then a bridge above the rock infested waters
of the Tennessee River
nearly seven years ago and eight years after her death.
Separate instances in Knoxville as I contemplated suicide.
Not yet diagnosed as bipolar
with a mentally ill brain trying to commit cerebral homicide.

I heard / sensed her Southern, slightly Ebonics accent,
"Girl, what the hell are you doin'? This ain't it."
I walk/ed away from the ledges.

I am thirty-one. I sink to the bathroom floor; towel loosely wrapped
around my anxiety-riddled body.
Dry heaves scratch frantically at my constricted throat.
The meager food in my stomach begins to sour.
On the lowest shelf of a cabinet, I see—
through blurred, glassy, green eyes—
the perfume my grandmother wore.

I set aside the undrank bottle of Sheldrake rosé
and remove the faux gold-plated White Diamonds cap,
inhaling slowly, deliberately
as best I can through congested nasal passages.

I feel Grandma Carolyn's nails again
against the soft skin of my childhood.
A John Wayne picture plays. I hear
the smoker's rasp of her low, yet sweetly
feminine timbre as she
whispers into my ear.

The bottle of wine remains sealed.
The tears resume but, this time,
more controlled, more quietly, more accepting.
Partly, in missing her.

Once upon a time, I was religious. I once bowed
my unshaven head, cast my eyes to the ground,
dropped a less broken body free of tattoos,
knelt with less damaged knees to pray.

I once talked to the sky
in the chance the heavens existed
and held her spirit.

Presently, I perform soliloquies
internally for her / me.

Wild Thing

He reflects
(up)on the sun and moon
rise and set
in her sometimes blue, sometimes green eyes,
and the stars shine
in her black irises
encircled with golden yellow-flecked tinges.

He believes the flowers
are painted by consuming kisses
from the pinkish red
tint of her lips
and the sunflowers replicate
her summer-honeyed brown tresses.

To him—in the landscape and skies;
oceans, rivers, streams;
flora, fauna, wildlife;
water fire
earth air—
she is there,
here, everywhere.

Coming out of the closet,

after twenty-eight years of existence
and seven years of knowing, to my parents.

I burn chiggers
with the smoking ends
of American Spirit cigarettes.

Carmine pinpricks against
grey, graffitied concrete.
Bright red parasites smoldered
to black—
a subconscious act;
my hand moving anatomically;

my body disconnected
from the illness-riddled brain in a head
heavy but on straight;
a mind that rolls roils riots,

but a heart steadily beating.

Ready/reluctant
to share an innate piece
of who I am:
shamelessly undeniably bisexual
unquestionably as is
my diagnosed bipolarity.

It is okay to exist
in your way & place on the spectrum
of sexuality.

Unfortunately,
at the time,
my mother and father did not agree

Fortunately,

as of late,
we see each other clearly.

The world might be a little better

if mothers and fathers loved their
daughters burgeoning from infants, toddlers,
childhood to adolescents to
adulthood—evolv/ed/ing and adopt/ed/ing individualistic,
self-cultivated beliefs, ideas, dreams, desires—
the bloomed version
of her nuclear esse in existence since creation
in the womb.

"Toss me in the water,
daddy, farther farther farther!"

We are the daughters
you once did unconditionally
carry, support, adore,
proud/loudly yell "that's my girl!"

You are unable to and / or disinterested
in understanding her
the more she is (re)acquainted with, relishes,
thinks, speaks for,
loves
herself.

My mother and father, once again,
proudly whoop
"that's my [daughter]!"

If you're wondering (how?),
therapy works wonders.

The barefoot stubbed toe in the dark

on stained oak
wrenched from its roots carved into
something
'useful,'

as I tell you a poem I wrote is to be published

and you ask
"in *The New Yorker*?"

"What?
Of course not,"
I stammer.

The jolt
to the ulna, stumbling fall
into the corned edge of drywall; nothing
humorous except for the lingering
reverberation in the bones of the humerus.

The plaqued teeth, prickly leaving,
missing a shoe, no goodbye, smeared
mascara and dirty underwear,
of a one-night stand.

Six years now since
(uncertain of the month and day |
but not of the vinyl scratch-skip-loop silence)
ongoing suspension, suspicion
sarcastic or sincere?

Unsure—you or me?—
for the blood-filled balloon in my sternum,
expanding unbursting,
full of the not being
good enough for

?

I am sure / enough at 31 years,
4 months, & 26 days
as the record spins and plays
and stays
steady.

for the first time,

not the first heartbreak,
instead of the crimson
vitality
trickling from a body
starv(el)ing by anxiety
in swirls down the shower drain

is the bright purple
of hair dye. A sign of change,
a coping mechanism
altering but in a way
only semi-permanently/-permeating
and undamaging intens(e)ity
greenish blue hued
dirty blonde strands

in lieu of shredded flesh
and a wreckage of scars
along wrists, hips, thighs
left
behind

Self-inflicted story/lines

I sit cross-legged on the lush living room rug
I would have slept on if I didn't need and want,
at times, the privacy of a closed door
from the other six people in my parents' home.
Two of whom are nine and eight years old.

My feet are cozied in my mother's fuzzy, red socks with white polka dots.
My body warmed by my father's vintage faded, navy-blue Russell Athletic sweatshirt.
My spine length dirty blonde hair woven into a low braid.

My mom comes up, crawling on her hands and knees,
to where I sit just in front of the carved stone of the fireplace.
I am half-reading a nonfiction collection of stories
and half-watching a college football game
on this holiday-frosted Saturday afternoon.
My dad is in the woods, waiting and watching
for deer to gun down.

She grabs my face between
her cold, rigid(ly) Raynaud's-riddled hands, but softly
as you would expect a mother's hands to be.
She smiles and manages
"I love you, do you know that?"
before her lips tremble, and tears peep
out from her eyes, slide down high cheekbones.

She holds my left arm gently between her piano player fingers.
She rolls up the too-big-for-me sleeves just shy of revealing the three long, thick,
still angry red,
diagonal scars slashed in lines across my wrist.
The marks are raised and cause my skin to stretch uncomfortably.
She rubs the small tattoo—
a simple cross with two feathers just below the palm of my hand—
with her thumb lightly.

"Do you want to get your scars fixed?"

Her bright blue eyes are so melancholy

and careful I think my heart may fracture.

I do/did not answer her question, but,
offer a quip tinged with a mix of dark humor
and the kindness to dry her tears.

Ten years later, more scars pockmark
my skin: indented, rounded cigarettes butted burns dotting upper thighs;
a red-lipped puckering scar of a third-degree burn;
thin white cicatrices on ribcage and hips;
hidden raised pigmented lines at neck's nape.

My body will not be 'fixed'
but will remain a creased map
lined with roads and trails,
marked with points of interest,
journeyed, to journey, journeying on,

but at a crossroads,

and I choose the road (I've) less traveled
leaving my scalpel
at the fork.

Gutted

I read poetry,
watch, listen
to what reminds me
and guts me like a fish.
Slice, scrape, scoop
eviscerated heart, bowels, organs, gills
spill
until emptied.

Each time
the knife
does not slide
as deeply
and cuts away less
less less until fleshy
scales steel then fragment
what once impacted
me

Kintsugi

Stretched, sinewy skin sealing in muscle,
bone, tendons, organs, blood pumping vessels.
A soft, clay embryo molded by my mother's womb

and my parents' careful hands
from infancy into childhood to adolescence
to the age of (ostensibly reciprocal) consent
and an underdeveloped prefrontal cortex.

I am seventeen:

a glacé centerpiece setting in the sun's gaze,
cocooned in the warm blaze / embrace
of her ki(l)n. Im/perfect ceramic artistry, as are all bodies.

This skull held this brain hid an imperceptible, persistent,
sinister divot in its neurological composition.

A sudden, singular incidence
s n a p p e d
underfoot of (some)one('s) poor decision
hatches and spreads the mental illness

as I leave permanently unnesting

and   s
          h
             a
               t
                 t
                   e
                     r .

I am eighteen:

my stout base filled to bursting, not with flowering bouquets, but disease, weeds,
invasive species, foreign unwelcome entities:
1. David feeds me cyclobenzaprines chased by Four Lokos and

whiskey.
He is twenty-three. Arrington Hall. Fifth floor in his room, top bunk.
2. An ex-boyfriend drives and disposes of my liquor-poisoned body
at the front door of a senior's frat house. Kenny, "Want something to
[in your] drink?"

I am twenty:

frequent ideation and attempts at suicide.
Malleable wrists, hips, thighs disfigured by fettling;
red eyed cigarette ends snuffed out against
ashtray skin. Trip after trip to the campus hospital, rushed in
after d(r)owning (in) Miller High Life and
whiskey and snorted Vicodin.

I am twenty-one:

at The Hill Bar & Grill in Knoxville, Tennessee.
The blow of my incensed fist (is)
broken by a glossy, oaken countertop. Intoxicated, again.
A bathroom mirror and stall door wrenched
u n h i n g e d.
I tread asphalt and un/consciousness,
squeezing a shard of a broken Jack Daniels bottle,
drawing pinpricks of DNA
from October-chilled, colorless fingertips.

A 911 call is made; by whom, I cannot say.
"You can accompany us to jail or voluntarily
go with the EMTs to the suicide ward," someone—
outfitted in a navy uniform—intonates kindly but sternly.
A smudged memory blurring displayed in my mind.

Awakening, as if coming up for air but still suffocating,
from alcohol-induced, anterograde amnesia
strapped to a gurney in a whirring ambulance.

A L O N E

save for two young, empathetic paramedics.

My shattered shards loosely gathered
and tethered by a sterilized, white, blue speckled gown,
then discarded onto a crisp-linened hospital bed
in a forgotten, deserted corridor of the suicide ward.

Solitarily confined and lonely
except for the night shift nurse (mis)treating
the middle-aged meth head, in the cot to my left, and me
as coldly as the spotlessly clean, white-tiled floor
is to our thinly socked feet.
This strung-out woman and I united in our lack of dignity,
naked toxin-filled bodies,
and stripped of our belongings.

Upon release,
as the sun crested the Rocky Top horizon,
I began the practice of Kintsugi:
the Japanese art of mending pottery.
Brushes dipped in lacquer mixed
with powdered gold, silver, platinum
to repuzzle the rough / incongruent /
jagged pieces, sculpting and smoothing
brokenness, into a renewed / repaired / reshaped composition.

I am twenty-two:

"We believe you have Bipolar I," my primary doctor hypothesized;
my therapist, Dr. Smart, theorized;
my psychiatrist, Dr. Romano, concluded with a decided diagnosis.

I am twenty-five:

3. My cocaine addicted/dealing, alcoholic, child-abused boyfriend.
His fist collides with the soft socket of my right eye, quickening
to a nightshade purplish blue. Handcuffed and forced into a police car. Steve
asks for a word. I concede, sure he will apologize, beg for forgiveness.
"Bail me out," he seethes through gritted teeth.

I am thirty:

the highest dose of Lamictal and 20 mg of Prozac daily aided

sometimes by Xanax and beta blockers.
Psychiatry; therapy; complete transparency with doctors, friends, partners, family;
positive coping mechanisms; virulent habits and relationships
repudiated. Efforts existing as the gold / silver / platinum-amalgamated
sealants to redress the recurring spider web of cracks, splinters, breakages
undertaken again and again and again
by the art of Kintsugi.

I am thirty, early June:

4. Dustin, a mutual friend. I crash at his place explicitly platonically.
Clear, continued recitations of no no no no NOnconsent.
He attempts to undress me, to touch my genitals and breasts.
I threaten him and exit slamming the door and stealing
his favorite sweatshirt on my way out. I (eventually) incinerate this remnant.

, July third:

5. Chris, a close friend of eight years. We elope
in lime green, donut-shaped floats
at Rabbit Run in Trumansburg, New York.
We "you may kiss the bride" then dunk one another,
baptizing and blessing our union
in the waters of my place of harmony and healing.

, July fifth:

Chris metamorphs; Dr. Jekyll to Mr. Hyde. A recessed
steel troffer thrown in a fit of rage gouges, scars, and bruises
my left shoulder. An eleven-hour, relentless
tirade of nocuous, vitriolic spittle hammered against the drums of my ears.

He: a cache of un/mismanaged mental health conditions
un & mistreated with a secret stash of scripts:
Xanax, Viagra, Prozac, Adderall, Klonopin.
Depression and anxiety, suicide ideation,
borderline personality disorder, intermittent explosiveness.
Drugs chased nonstop with chewing tobacco, weed,
and a disguised double Old Fashioned.

Undisclosed $10k in unpaid medical bills,

unemployment, and a (un)declared (to me) bankruptcy.
Hidden cameras, multiple break-ins. He and I bound legally only
by a governmental piece of paper; separated
wedding pictures by kitchen scissors
held in his bony hands,

separated

by my grandmother's Remington
shotgun barrel, my dog's bared teeth,
five-hundred fifty-two miles, and an order of protection.

,December eleventh:

a post episodic discovery—influenza can induce / advance
gold-flecked, splintered, reformed bodies
and illness-riddled minds / my / mine towards insanity.
Insom(a)nia plagued me for three nights
prior to contracting the flu. My temperature climbed
as the virus lit my cells and brain on fire.
I drifted in and out of sleep—
a restless stream of un/conscious fever dreams.

A bewilderingly dizzying   s h i f t   from waking
to a bluebird sky and a lawn snow laden beyond
frosted glass windows; in the crook of my arm, one dog
and one buried in my lap—

a vertigo imbalanced d e v i a t i o n

to all consuming, wayward worry; paranoia; choked crying;
nauseating, sometimes emetic anxiety; insecurity
as to what my re/actions may have de/constructed
and the wreckage left behind.

I am justified, I reason internally
as I drive by my partner's house t o r n

between

genuine worry for his safety

given rise by an unsent "I'm home" text,
after a late night out drinking
and suspicion weaving theories
in my rollercoastering mind
of with whom, where, and how he is cheating.

6. (addendum: he was,
but I will spare him the explicit
illicit content/context)

An hour later, knees curled to my chest.
Tear-glassed, reptilian green eyes
baptize the peeling vinyl steering wheel,
condensating the chipped windshield
in the frigidity of this twenty-two years
old Toyota Tacoma. "I'm sorry.
I know it was a crazy thing to do," texted apologizing.

I am thirty-one:

a third-degree burn, a puckered and blood/red-lipped,
one by two-inch fatty, gaping mouth branded into the dermis
of my left wrist by a blackened fire poker wielded
in my shadow-guided dominant (skeleton) hand (in the closet)
(unleashed in the [right] wrong circumstances).

In a cabin in the backwoods of Owego,
—alone—my laptop open to a many-tabbed search history
of the most efficient, swiftest means to die:
an ice-plated pond awaits nearby.

Hypothesis: suicide/cerebral homicide.

Theory: hypothermia.

Conclusion: unattempted
(a[n] [infinite/simal] win)
(eight years clean and counting).

A chronic illness,
an endless loop of (a) fleeting fix(es)

for what cannot be cured, but mended
by the art of Kintsugi
again and again and again.

I forgive myself—
to you (know who you are),
please forgive me as well.
I embrace the heartache
not as a breaking, but a heart shaping
experience,

readying for better things to come.
Fragmented pieces resealed
with gold-dusted lacquer
into a reshaped work of (he)art.

Foggy

For earlier today was clear
& the river was
unburdened & unmuddied

but, by evening, the sky gathers
cumulonimbus torrentially saturated rain clouds
deluging/diluting
into the night, into the
following day
& suddenly, everywhere, all things
are grey, drowned, & unblossoming.

Drowning

when you are fighting—
tendons, muscle, organs, every bodily fiber
—to swim, to keep your head above water.
A heart pulsing, bursting to stay afloat.
But an invisible,
malevolent, heavy hand on your spine
exists, shoving you under unendingly.

A tightly held rope coiled and snaking
around your larynx, trachea, and lungs.
You clutch at your throat—
tearing, searing flesh against woven hemp.
You push to resurface for a breath
to only be plunged again below
to the blinding gloom
of the asphyxiating waters of sorrow,
pain, heartbreak, grief,
unrelentingly.

Death seemingly
more and more welcome
in lieu of this ceaseless waterboarding.
He is pounding at the groaning door
of your will to live.

To(wards) relief or agony?
To sink or swim?
To be or not to be?

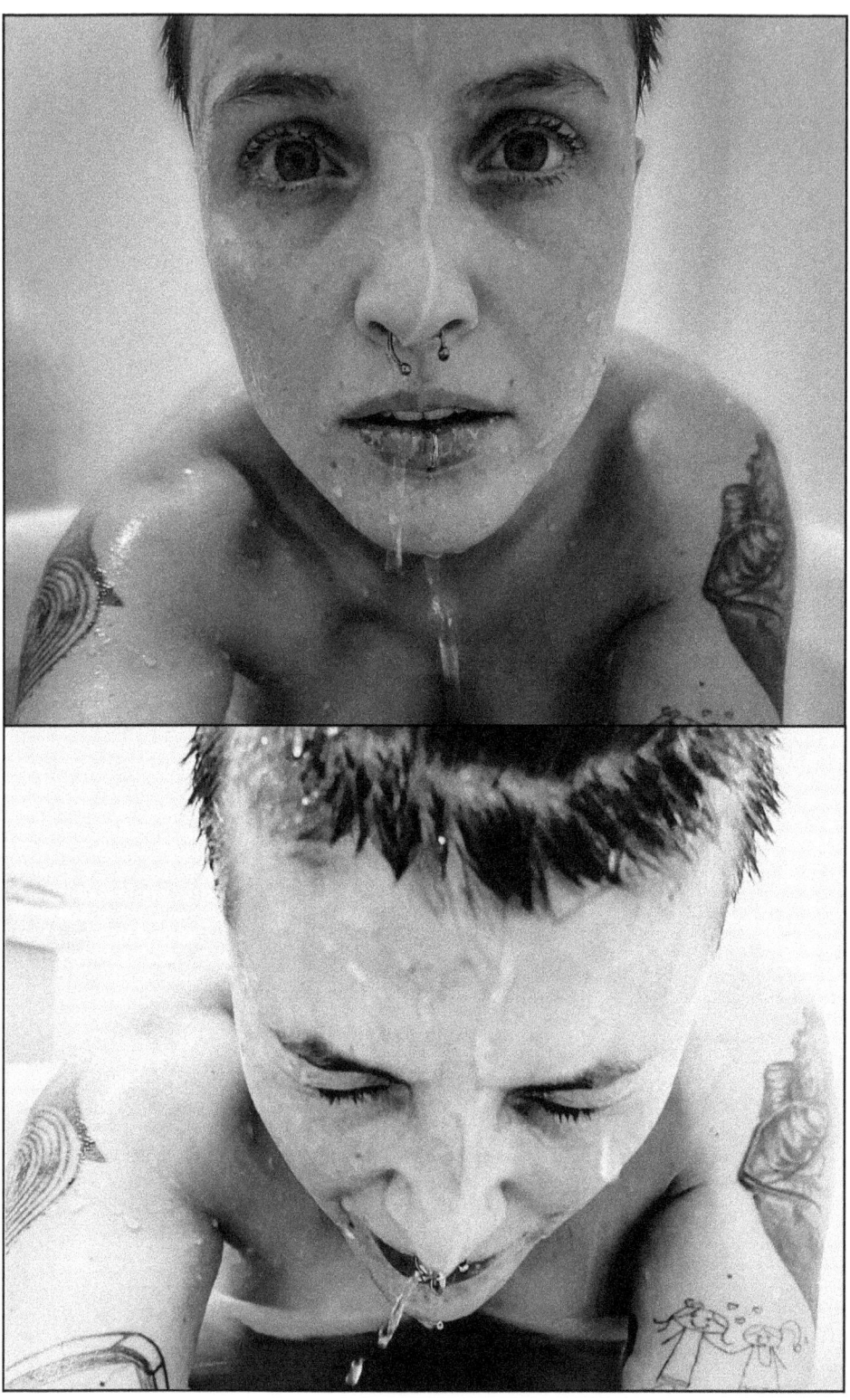

Rush hour

Lucky Charms for breakfast
she doesn't finish;
a Red Bull, Lamictal, Prozac,
and Xanax on the side,
and an unwashed apple
for her drive.

One hand on the wheel,
the other trailing smoke
from the window.
Rain stains the sleeve
of her grandpa's green
Army coat worn in Vietnam
black lettered surname "KNIGHT"
embroidered on the left breast pocket.

A playlist labeled "f*ck it all,"
but she just keeps skipping songs
of unmatched
misery miserably
lacking in kindred company.

A cacophony
of melancholy
intros,
and the click and hum
of her truck's
cassette player

as the anger
runs down
both cheeks
and into her ashtray mouth.

Epitomized

sometimes
what was wanted;
never what was needed.

Distinguished the self.
Warmed hands in the
wavering whispering waning
flame until the recognition,

red spot technique,
rouge test
is positive.

It was you; but,
with fabling eyes,
cannot see. Hole-punch, blood
to the mirror—not yours (?);
lucidly looking down
on the scene;

essence, innards gush, slop
left to putrescence,
but
it is too cold.

Unaccountable

You invite me to a Boombox show
at Iron Works in Buffalo.
A two-and-a-half-hour drive from home
on a Tuesday evening.
Work the following day and a ten o'clock morning meeting.

At the bar dancing and drinking until 11:30,
talking / laughing / smoking a shared clove cigarette
till 2 a.m. with your brother-in-law and sister.

You apologize for being sloppy.
Unminding, I giggle, smile, plant a kiss
on your rosied cheek.

You mandate leaving
in the morning at 7:30 a.m.
I suggest, playfully: *how 'bout we leave
maybe, thirty minutes, an hour, two hours later,
never and work remotely?*
You and I laugh. You smile at me and wink.

We go to bed. Your mood switches
in tandem with the overhead light bulb
as the latch catches on the door.
You say nothing, back turned to me.
My dog and I are already in the guest bed
drifting into sleep.

"I don't appreciate all the pushback
you were giving me about leaving early
and wanting to have a productive day."

Sobering yet still drowsy
a little tipsy, in response I stutter,
"I was mostly joking. It's fine.
We can leave whenever."

You slide under the sheets.
Your vibrations send aflutter—

in the bowels of my belly—
butterflies not of excitement but anxiety.
You don't touch me. You turn to face me,
somber and unspeaking.

"What?" I ask after a seeming eternity
of unbroken silent staring.

"I wasn't expecting to see Luna in the bed.
I thought the dogs would sleep in their crates."

"What? No. I didn't say that. Luna always sleeps with me."

You disagree wordlessly.

"I'm afraid I'm going to snore.
I'm going to keep you up again.
Another night of no sleep."

"I don't mind.
It's fine."

"I'm going to sleep on the couch,"
you mutter and did not hear /
you do not /
will not hear
what I have to say.

"You are upsetting me.
I thought we were fine," I sob.

You stare,

distantly,
and leave,

as tears
slowly well and trail down my cheeks.

I bury my face into the pillow.
I let both dogs sleep in the bed with me.

I awake earlier than you, pack my clothes and toiletries.
I walk the dogs. By 7 a.m., I am dressed, caffeinated, ready.

You grumble as the dogs greet you
on the couch to say good morning.

You are finally ready by 9 a.m.

We leave and ride in near silence—
a quiet that prickles against your skin.
Twists your organs. Pinches your lungs.

You sometimes speaking and me
answering only when a response is needed.

You do not apologize.
You do not seem to realize
what has been done.

I look ahead. Out of the window.
Anywhere but at you.
I blink the tears away. The tightness / the distance grows.

I had recently made a vow to never drink again if the stability
of my emotional state, mental health, or mood is in question.

But what happens,
when we are drinking,

and your fluctuating depression is
and your unpredictable mood is
and your lack of accountability is

the issue?

I wonder

does it strike you,
now,
the stupidity of
a filtered life?
It seems you dislike
it now
and then
noncommittal

I sometimes ponder
if it was me
then
influencing you
now
when I could not

before

the story reached
its end

I *was* sturdy

as a fixed wall,
but tired of
standing still
and you staring
listlessly so

I became a window
that you might see your/myself
more clearly
but I tired of
breaking and being broken;
and you
with nowhere to go
except to fall so

I became a door
that you might come through (for) me
but I tired of opening and closing,
being slammed and wrenched open so

I became an exit—
in case of emergency—
armed, alarmed, and locking
as it swings
shut

and you did not (re)turn
for a last glance
before you left.

Slam.

Narcotize

At six, fascinated
by Earth and its life.
He watched the sun/rise
each morning.

At twenty-six, obsessed
with caffeine and pornography.
He greets each day with a hard-on
and a cup of black coffee,
no sugar
and no cream

except the viscous fluid
on his hands, trembling from the fillip.

Misogynists take note

Young men experienc(e)ing(d) (in)
telltale-old-as-time masculinity
have no need of 'role models' but to (have) writ(t)e(n)
100 to 400 sonnets, *self*-disdains, or cazones
addressing a (misoginistically treated) cruel mistress
who is pen(to paper)etrating him with (hu)man-crafted arrows
from her fiery feminine(ist) eyes.

Betrayal

I was (r)ejected from the plane
suddenly & without warning,
utterly unequipped
for my rapid descent—
and gaining momentum—
to the hard Earth from a great height
on what was once cloud nine.

As I bulleted towards sure demise
& flailed & cried out for help, I looked up

to see you completely stoic & composed,
standing by the open door
before it closed.

Any(but) w(here)

Silence except
for quivering breath, with each
rise & fall of your chest

might have felt the tears
as each fell
had the black curled hair
not caught each and held fast
dew dropped on your thorax.

Might have felt
her lacking presence
had you not slept
so peacefully when
she could not.

Might have felt,
if the cavity there
between your pectorals,
was where
her head still laid to rest,

but instead,

she left.

To all the fish in the sea

Night brings
men to hook line and sink
me. Curved obstructions lodged deeply
hold fast for a short time.
The men yank their rods
and reel in
what is lodged inside,
gutting then tossing me back
in, deciding to pursue a better catch.

I go for the worm
I take the bait

again and again

and again

hoping to be a keeper

Limitless Interrogatives

You always say last
cigarette, just one more, one more
and you'll quit.
One more drag,
one more sip,
one more dance.

Then you return to consciousness
as your body metabolizes and flushes
the remaining toxicity.

You are sprawled out; your back
aching against something hard, something cold
(concrete?) in black shorts and an extra-large t-shirt
that you don't think you've
been acquainted with before.

But you're not sure.
You're never sure
about anything or anyone—anymore—
who just said my name and waved hello?

But you don't think you've
ever seen them before.
You can't find the jacket,
your mom bought you for
your eighteenth birthday.

And when she asks you why you never wear it,
you say *I do, just not around you.*
I do, I just forgot it in my dorm room.
I do, I just . . .

but only because you're not sure.

What happened?
What happened?

I'm not sure.

my mind begs the question

"why do you keep doing this to yourself?"

my heart w(ishes)hispers
"maybe this time."

my soul, pleadingly on behalf of each,
"please."

maybe there will be a day
all three will say
"no" to maybe.

"Oh lawd"

I finish smoking a spliff, high on clouds of marijuana
just before joining a video conference
to teach a graduate school class.
I am drinking a margarita poured from
a plastic bottle with a twist off cap,
pre-mixed and disgusting
in a chipped cocktail glass.

The tap water on Podunk Road, even filtered,
tastes as nasty as this blood alcohol content increasing libation
but does not have the same effect
on the consciousness.
My body is currently ninety-eight percent
liquor and weed and, maybe,
one percent water, caffeine,
bodily fluids, and a bowl of Lucky Charms cereal
from the convenience store down the street.

I receive,
at 7:49 p.m., a text
from the one I loved and he lost. No context.

> *Will I lose $100 tonight and cement*
my legacy as a terrible gambler, or will I
win only to lose it all at a later date?

> *You will do both.* I reply.

No response; months pass.

A late, post-midnight, drunk text
from the one who requested exclusion
then cheated.

> *This song slaps. I like it.*
I added it to my drums playlist.
It is reminiscent
of our moments together. I miss
being together. Don't you agree?

> *Yeah? Why is that?* I reply
disagreeably.

No response; weeks pass.

"Oh lawd," I hear my Grandma
breathe silently loud in my mind's ear.
I smile;
been a while
since I heard you(r)
southern-drawled, cigarette-smoky voice
here, there, anywhere.

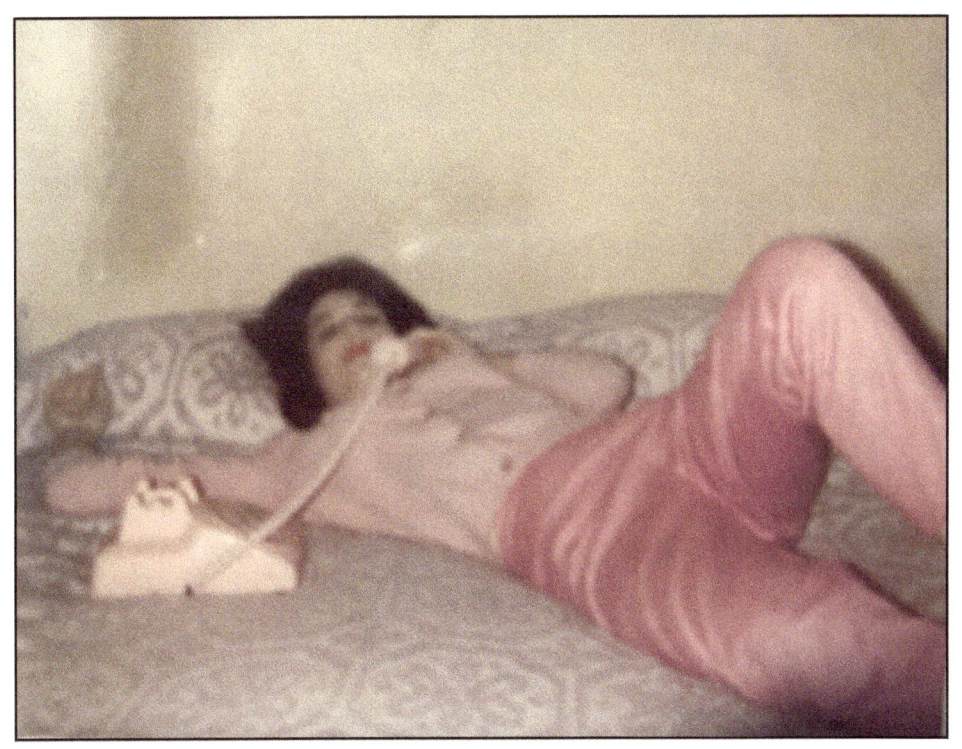

Punctuate

Carved lines on their faces, but
not the parentheses
drawn by "I love you"s.

The skin just below his Polo shirt
collar smells of soap
and slightly soured milk
to match the anemic tint of his pale skin.

He stares owl-eyed
with knotted fists, his feet
on the coffee table.
His breathing, rock candy
breaks, crumbles, with each snap and grind
of his quivering jawline.

The conversation begins,
but his mouth isn't moving,

nor is hers—only a line
of flat landscape darkening
as the sinking sun unseen

through bluish black clouds
carries the promise of thunderous,
stormy din
rolling in with the coming
twilit sky.

Unwelcome return

back to monotony
and not eating
when no one is here to
see
how you are doing
to smell the nicotine-
tinged tobacco breathing
preoccupy your thinking.
back to waking up
too late
inside of
a silence of the third degree.
back to a drawn out noxious drag
with half a cup of coffee
forgetting the rest till it is cold
and your morning dose
of antineurotics and listless
staring.
back to falling asleep
too early to
static and toned down
brightness from the TV
as your only company.
back to crawling to your knees
bouncing back to your feet,
standing in unsteady fragility
instead of staying steady.

Disassociating

stubby fingers ending in anxiety
bitten nails on the keys typing typing typing
thinking thoughts racing gathering spilling
chaotically
jumping task to task to task to
nothing is complete/d

twisting tugging the septum piercing
hooped through soft nasal cartilage;
biting, tonguing the stainless steel threaded
through labrum tissue:
twinges in efforts to be free
from nightmarish lucid daydreaming.

a *ping*,
the phone screen glows
three photos sent
from my seventeen-year-old sister.
A text request
for my uninformed opinion
as to >*which purse?*
knowing I have zero fashion sense,
am not trendy or 'with it,'
and have not carried a purse since
I was ten.

I smile and openly laugh
at the fact she is asking
me, of all people.

I vote for the last option
despite knowing you (so well)
will buy the one I like least.

> *Thanks, sissy.*

> *I appreciate you asking me
but I don't know if I'm the
most reliable purse source.*

Why did you ask me?

I can hear and see, in my head,
her laughing too.

> I know but I wanted your opinion!

grounding me.

Deactivated

i'm going away
but will leave you with this:

we are on the losing end
of an information war.
don't talk, don't listen,
lay [keep] your head [down]
on my shoulder

Cheers

to all the nights
still / silent as should be
but leave the mind chattering
against fang-toothed thoughts submerged in icily
distant dreams
of what is out of reach.

Des(in)spite (of)
the self-help you read;
the shrinks you see;
the pills you swallow, gagging;
the meditation you practice;
the self-medicating
you seek; the philosophy, astrology, prophecy
you heed,

the softest
space is now
the hardest:

the monsters are now under the sheets.

Malaise

Pallid skin
stretching over
creaking bone
waning muscle mass and tone;

a body atrophying.
Losing weight
and substance
(un)naturally.

*I worry
about you,*
he texts
what he
doesn't mean.

I gobble it up.
Hungry for you(r words that) / what cannot fulfill
me. Bellyaching for any morsel
proffered from your hands
caught redhandedly.
It's all I can stomach,
and it's not much,
and it's slipping,

thinning,
d w i n d l i n g.

Unmotivation

White, round pills
tasting of alum powder,
and stagnant clock hands.
Words mellow into refrigerator humming,
forgotten slices of pizza,
and a carton of milk
spoiling over the weekend.
No car horns, barking dogs, sirens,
train whistles, voiced voices

here

just the disappointment of rain
on the window pane.

Bird Dog Whiskey

The letters from her—
sent but unread—
piled in the drawer,
next to his bed.

She materialized one morning,
unanticipated/unannounced
except for a soft knock at our apartment door
on a cold, hangover-free Saturday;
the sun hung in the blue northener sky
after a drunken night.

I watched, through the peephole,

a funhouse mirror distortion:

he leaned into her;
she pressed her petite finger to
the stubbly meat of his clefted chin.
He smiled to keep her eyes dry,

at the expense of mine.

I walked away. I poured a drink.
Kept the bottle in my hand.
I read the letters she wrote.

My mouth and throat dry
as if a cat
had crawled in with the drop
of my jaw and died.

I wa(o)ndered until I (was) lost

Too little, too late

I will not
exist in a folder
for when you miss it.
I will watch you delete
the pics.
I refuse to reside
in your weekend away,
not your home.
I will not be an aside
where I was once the soliloquy
you spoke.
I will not be the sometimes,
the other,
the then, the maybe.

If I cannot be the one,
I will not be anyone
to you

except perhaps the
items left behind or

the gathering
dust,

but those things are not me,
and I am not those things.

You say you have your memories,
but, to you,
—remember?—
this was/is short-term.
Seconds was/is all its worth.

5, 4, 3, 2,

g(one)

I am folded,

origamically,
into a shape of unspeakable
exhaustion and yet
cannot grasp sleep.
I slip
and wedge
into a cleft
between

tendon/muscle/joint/mentally/bone-weariness

and

insomnia

dreading the subconscious

and the resurgence to consciousness

Fool's gold

You don't believe in fate

I want to write to

you

write to me and say:

*if it's meant to be,
could be a shot one day*

leaving me
hanging on hope
until the rope's end
catches the breath
in my tight throat

because
a buried memory survives
starved in the recess of my mind—

you refuting *meant to be*

Antidote

A monster imprisoned
as a false sense of security,
rattling the vessels
of rib-caged throbbing flesh.
The creature snaps snarls shrieks
for unleashment
from the anatomical depths
in a recess
of ominous thoughts, resentfulness,
toxic tempestuousness, hostility,
vengefulness, vindictiveness.

The clawing sharply ungulated beast
tearing at a healing heartened organ
pumping coagulant to suture tattered fragments.
The unyielding shadow
slithering through still infected fissures
caused by un- & collateral damage.
Unforgiving. Unrelenting.
Sinister. Savage.

When
a moment of heartbreak
releases the horror—

buried undiscovered until the
oft repeated three atomic words stated sincerely:

"*I am sorry*"

are, for the first (in a life)time, accepted fully.
The terror once holed away in the darkest corners
of a once debilitated body freed.
A moment of absolute(ion) unshackling.

The strangulating black vapor spewed;
the cloud of venomous parasites expelled;
the murder(ous) of crows flew;
the rotten, poisoned souring sustenance retched

from a mouth honeyed by
three antidotal, antiseptic words.
A breath(e) in; and breath(e) out:

"I *forgive* **you**."

you took me swimming

in the frigidity of a partially
iced over Cayuga Lake.
You were going in
for a brisk dip—a daily tryst even in winter—
and dared me to/o.

I couldn't resist,
despite being accustomed to the sticky
humidity and warm waters of Florida, Georgia,
southern Virginia, North Carolina, Tennessee.
Denim jeans, an ex's t-shirt, Doc Martens,
and bodily insecurities forgotten
on the slick rocks of the water's edge.

I stood, exposed skin,
but my breasts, genitalia, and buttocks
hidden beneath boy short panties
and a sports bra. The unshaven hair on my thighs
bristling in the October chill.

I am swaddled in two semidry towels—
smelling only slightly soured—in your truck—
a Toyota Tacoma twins with mine but in white;
and cozied in your fleece-lined flannel
jacket given, not lent.

We shared and drank straight
from the bottle of wine unearthed
in a cellar on the campus of the university.
Intoxicated on fermented fruit
and hours of unabashed, candid conversating.

A first kiss between our chapped lips
as you grabbed
my chin gently
in your calloused hands
and drew my rosy-cheeked face
towards you.
I came and stayed willingly

until I couldn't.

The jacket was returned,
but **I** *didn't*

until you re-emerged
broke the surface
and pulled my life (self)preserved
body to shore

Upstate Mid-September

The nights are cooler now
in Upstate New York, frosting over the
remnants of summer.

We are walking the dogs.
You stop. I can barely see
your form—opaque in the cloak of darkness only
the countryside can afford.
All six feet of muscular, lean, farm boy body
stoops down as
you bend your sun leathered face
to the dew gathering grass.

"Thought I saw a firefly,"
you mutter
as you continue through
the wheat field. Cinders shake from the spliff
in your left hand—my dog's leash in your right—
embers flying orange and bright
like ashen, late lingering fireflies.

Requited

Arrived with no
expectations;
actually, without a clue
of what
I'd say, you'd say, we'd say,
I'd do, you'd do, we'd do.

But last night
left you
left me
left us
with a suitcase full

of words
shook from your lips
the "I didn't know"
was what
I knew all along
and the *felt*
was what
I had been waiting with

each day after day
over two & a half years,
thinking I knew
I'd never hear / feel / receive /
requited from you

you're somethin' else

he is in a white pickup truck
he is tall
with blond curls
I message to the woman
from whom he is collecting
a box of books
for me,

he is sturdy, stalwart,
(to my five-foot four form) towering;
hitting his Herculean mandible
are sun-bleached blond and brown ringlets
I loop around my fingers
wrapped around his.
I call him a demigod;
his canine fanged smile indescribable
to be witnessed
and not the same
full of unsaid unnecessary words
between us

I want to say

you can't miss him
I couldn't
the first time I saw him

but she won't comprehend

so I describe him
as she might see him
because she won't see him
like I do, cliche
adjectives unjustified
in their simplicity

because no one sees
my emerald eyes
only for him

his sky blues clearly
only for me

I love you

Lowercased letters, tiny words
only a breath, just one, to utter

gasp in, shudder, *whoosh* out.

Softly, not yelled, a whisper.
Those bite with an iron jaw:
a hickey
on your heart.

A love mark
that swells and purples,
spreads and sets in.

My love language is

biting.

Grounded

She sees
the summits of mountains,
where land meets sky,
in his chestnut eyes
and the eternal expanse
variegated with
the orange red and golden
leaves of Autumn
in the deepness of his pooled irises.

She believes his stalwart hands
tenderly sculpted each
rock and tree,
believes the gentle and shy
creatures mimic his spirit
and his joyous tears—shed with her—
and those of heartbreak before—shared with her—
swelled the rivers, lakes, streams, seas,
where water and earth meet.

For her, in the Summer sun-rayed sky,
in the gales of Fall, in the serenity granted
of a Wintery snow-blanketed
world, in the cheery conversating
of robins and swallows returned for Spring,

he is here, there,
everywhere.

Wordless Chorus

The first time I sang, wholly unrestrained, a/loud(ly)
with each breath from my asthmatic lungs,
in front of another human:
we were cross-legged on the gnarled wooden floor
in the dead of night in your living room.

You were enfolded in my arms
as you startlingly howled
the lyrics in harmony with Jim James
spinning on the record player.

I longed to be so free,
toss my head back and siren scream
'oooo hooo,' along with you to the "wordless chorus."

I did and, again,
I owe/d to you
another disentombed
vulnerable unbridled

piece of me

Written/in-between

sleeps
with Sarah Shook
and Jim James ringing
in my ears.
In between the lines
of un and consciousness
on a bus rattling on

to another place
I can't call home /

another place
you do not exist

"I ain't. We will."

The smallest words,
the shortest phrase,
the silence, the pauses,
the unspoken conversating
between bodies
and the eyes
drink your breath away.

Humming her tune on and on
her rhythm replays,
repeatedly, inside his head
devouring skin, bones, tendons,
muscles, organs, soul.

Nothing stays the same;
everything's gonna change;
that's what they say,

but tho(e)se two (uh huh)
will remain. One million love(r)s
unlike us / ours.
Found, lost and found again, lost.

Her impression in his bed.
His heart in my lap
his hand on my thigh
and unbroken eyegazing

leaning in
to the cold night.
Bare feet over a pitted fire
burning shin and ankle
twice, unnoticed till morning,

moving to the forefront
back into to the light,

slowly

but, *hey, we got time.*

You called

and spoke with words
I cannot summon
to my restless mind.

Waking at 4:02 am,
right hand to my ear;
a smile still
lilts the edges
of my lips.

I feel the shift
as I drift
out of un- to consciousness.

My phone lies still and silent
on the nightstand to my left
with its undeniably blank face.

Only the soft noise of the television
still playing
has anything to say to me.

Mattress on a concrete
floor
in the unfinished basement
bachelorette pad in my parents' home.

No privacy but, in the deadness
between night and morning, only
the concrete walls witness
my pillow muffled, sobbing scream

for this waking nightmarish dream.

Dreamt of you.

I cannot recall the details—
the two of us in bed at a hotel?
vacationing maybe—

fading

just like you, starting to,

but I was laughing and so were you.
I laughed aloud so fully
I awoke as if from nightmare-driven screams.

3:12 am on the couch
in my soon-to-be not my house:

moving boxes, blank walls,
furniture for sale or marked for donation,
emptiness, loneliness, sickness
and a toilet full of
bile from anxiousness.

The first and only time in my life,
I have woken up from laughing
(false mirth evolving into sobbing).

I'll go back to sleep, try
maybe I'll find
you there again

keep on dreaming.

say(ing) what you (don't) mean

> how is it? in Michigan?

> great

> That great, huh?

*> You said you were coming.
Said you would visit me this week.*

> I said I'd try.

Did you?

I didn't ask you to;

you offered.

Unfortunately
you still don't say what you mean
don't do what you say

hypocrisy
and dishonesty the only
flaws I refuse to label
as mistakes.

Personality traits
devoid of development?
Genes I did not inherit?

Addendum to Antidote

Twelve hours
after returning from vacation,
you text:

> *We need to talk.*

Four words, even in writing,
sparking heartattacking uneasy disquiet
in my squirming stomach
and retching dry heaving against
my uvula.

You walk in the door,
you keep your distance—
no hug hello or the usual kiss,
work boots stay laced, your jacket still
draped over your upper body.

I say:

"Hi. You wanted to talk?"

"Yeah. I can't do this anymore."

"Can't do this? You mean dating?"

"Yeah. I'm sorry" as you move past
me to gather your things.

"It was fun . . . while it lasted"
is all I can manage.

I help you, wordlessly,
carefully placing each item
into reusable tote bags—once filled
with our houseplants, board games, Christmas gifts,
Halloween costumes, groceries—

until I am entirely

debilitated by uncontrollable crying.
I sink to the floor shivering
in shocked denial
quickening to a sickening
souring of the veggie burger in my belly.

I hear the side door's hinges grind
and see your six-foot-six silhouette
disappear from view behind
the window pane. The solitary silence
crackles like radio static.

My heart skips one, two, three
beats of disbelief before I run to the door.

All that remains are tire tracks reversing
out of the muddied driveway
and your spare key
discarded on the washing machine.

> We ain't friends?

What then?

Your southern ease coming
through easily
even in
written words.

> An ex?

A large, blood red
X slashes my vision.
A mistake to be edited, fixed
or entirely erased.
Two syllables twang against
threadbare heartstrings.
I wince.
It has been a while since
your words have bitten.

> I love you. Bye.

then ask again
> Why can't we be friends?

I start and stop and start
and stop responding.

Only wrong words to write
that *can't be* but are (al/l)right.

If she only knew
the wrongness of the
words you write to me,

but I will not be the one to say.

Di(e)spa(i)rity

between you /
me /
your love /
mine:

how easily you
fall asleep
when I reach
out, distress
signaling
capitalized letters
white text
against a bubble of blue

> *I HAVE TO
GET OUT OF HERE.*

Three hundred and eighty miles away

and you haven't heard
from me
in days.

*   *   *

How my breathing
catches and sticks
in the pinched crevices
of concern-constricted lungs
at the appearance of a sad emoticon
in a bubble of gray
under your name.

> *Are you ok?*
I text in response
almost immediately

three hundred and eighty miles away,

and I won't hear
from you
for days

I walk home;

clear plastic cup of white
wine in one hand,
thrift store tweed coat in the other
wanting to feel cold
and craving a cigarette.

A young woman walks by;
smoke billows
from the Marlboro Red she holds
between her bluish lips.

Couples climb in
and out of taxis
home.

I suck in shards of air
and blow out clouds
of steaming oxygen pretending /
wishing for the noxiousness
of tobacco and nicotine.

I walk alone

wanting to be cold.

Lonely Sound

Her boots unheeded
next to the door,
(she'll not need
them anymore),
just socks to shield
her toes and feet
from the gelid concrete.

A way to find her,
reach her,
left on the kitchen counter, forgotten.
The unrelenting arms
of wind beseeched her
to go back in.
She shouldered against
it through the metal handed doors.

The branded-in cold
from the railroad ties
seized all warmth from her
naked thighs.

One minute
after she
returned from outside
(giving in to pleas
of thirty-below air) with dried
tears and red cheeks—
the door yawning open
without resistance—
she hears the whistle
of a train cry out, the grinding
metal-to-metal pounding
the night, moaning
that lonely sound.

She thinks
just in time,

her heart throbs
just a little too late.

Unhaunted

I no longer hear his
white trash, backwoods West Virginian accent
lilted with (mis)appropriated Southern charm
camouflaging an unhinged,
un/mismanaged mind
asphyxiating in a noxious cloud
of medications prescribed
unknowingly by a handful of doctors
and taken spasmodically and ill advisedly.

I no longer see his
features comprehensibly.

Fragments distorted:

a sharply pointed nose
overly large for
such a thin, horsey face,

black hair thinning in places
and combed over a balding pate,
publicly concealed under a baseball cap,

too small, unremarkable
blue? green? brown? eyes cloudy
and glazed by Jim Beam whiskey
in a stainless-steel travel mug disguised as coffee.

A puzzle, missing pieces
discarded intentionally,

subsiding exponentially into two dimensional
jigsaw-puzzled—incomplete—resemblance

fading fading fading into existential nonexistence.

Play with at your own risk.

"You'll be sorry," he said
before he turned
to leave and looked directly
into my anole green irises
offset by red veined white sclera.

"I won't be," I said staring
back defiantly, despite the brokenness
of my body and a disheartened organ plummeting
when he shoved me
from the cliff's edge, called it quits,

and deserted me as I stood on the next ledge
from which I eventually walked away led by
my own trembling hand (in hand).

My therapist sincerely
took the (unsaid) (right) words right out of my mouth:
"I am sad for him, not you.
But I am sad for the situation he put you in(to).
He did and does not know
who you are despite your openness.
You offered a (wholly) true story
he could have been a part of (partner) (in)—
he's an idiot, honestly.
For that and for him, I feel sorry."

I start by tellin' all my best stories first,
then entrust to you all of my worst—
a much longer list of stor(i)ed grievances—
just so you know what you've
signed up for, what you're gettin' yourself into,
and who you're dealin' with.

I'll be the girl
you (chose) were chosen
to deserve.

I once knocked back alcohol until my consciousness

evanesced (in)to blundering blurred blackness.
Often, suffering the subsequent sunrise to sunset
disassociation, anxiety, mania, vomiting, and/or yacking
on poor decision(s)-making.

I once ingested Benadryl 'til I read
aloud from my college Linguistics textbook
in a manner starting with each ending letter
to each starting letter of each word.

The professor asked me to leave
he *asked* me to leave
you asked me to leave

I left then swallowed more of those
25 L479 imprinted, pink pills—
too much, too much, it was all much too much,
and I had to have my stomach pumped,
was told I was lucky
(brain whispering *in your opinion*)
to have survived.

I once was a late out at night owl sneakin'
into the community pool
waking up hungover to teach at Sunday school.
You woulda found me, behind the dumpster out back,
holding class for the choir boy
who made eyes at me as he passed
our church pew and saw me pre(a)ying on my knees.

All the toxins, the drugs, the liquor,
and the bodies offering only emptiness
have become boring to me,

so now, everywhere is clear/ly better,

and *that* is *everything.*

I am the *woman*
you (chose) were chosen
to deserve

when I reached the verdict
that you were and are and always will be
guilty
of not deserving *me*.

Rabbit Run Rd.

The Taughannock Creek leads
to Cayuga Lake feeding constantly
its water to a larger body. The stream
turns a bend out of sight underneath
a bridge on which cars pass noiselessly.

Here,/hear the rush of the water/falls
down carved rock faces muffling all sound
save for the plane soaring overhead on to its
next destination and the warbling and twittering
of birds returned for Spring.

The water is clear and glints strands of sun rays
where the bottom is uneven and moves in dips and waves.
Starbursts of light—like those that pop behind your ocular lenses
with a 1, 2 uppercut punch or that dance at a sparkler's end—
glitter off the surface. The bluish grey rock slabs are flat, yet dimpled,
and warm themselves basking in the bluebird sky.

As the light of day fades, or in early mornings

as the light rises, you can hear the high-pitched jingles
of peepers returned from hibernating.

You might see (or hear) herons, hawks, falcons,
osprey, geese and goslings, a number of song birds.
Two ring-necked ducks—a couple—
rustle the water as they fly to the lower, deeper belly
of the stream searching for prey, diving under and dunking
their heads, black feathers glistening.

You might see a fisher—as I did once—
or river otters.
We spotted a young male beaver
surveying the area to decide
upon a dammed home of his own.
I get close enough to touch him
but seat myself to his right awed at our closeness.

I observed a chocolate brown coated mink
slyly traversing downstream ducking underneath
exposed tree roots and moving slowly. I watch him
until he disappears from sight, wending
around the creek's bent knee.

We spotted a young red fox
traveling downstream on the far embankment.
On his return upstream, he was hightailing it
along the edge of the forest
tracked closely by two crows, nearly nipping at his paws.

You will see so many fishes and crawfish,
thousands of tadpoles, and hundreds of tiny frogs
smaller than the marble-sized rocks.
You might see a snake slither among
the brush along the bank or across the water.

You will assuredly see these things
if I spot them. I will call to them and, sometimes,
carefully catch them. Holding them gently
for a few moments,
before returning them.

You will always see me.
I am always here.
More than any other person
and more than any other place.
Even in Fall and Winter.
Nearly daily in Spring and Summer.

It is my respite
offering, always, a healing
much needed.

I come here alone
to edit, read, and write
as it offers the much needed
clarity, quiet, silence.

Here, I can fall asleep more easily
and quickly than in any bed
with my back flat against a rock
and perhaps a towel for my head.

I come here
and return
and stay as long as the sun
is hung in the sky.

I hope this for you—
to have a sanctuary of/fering
similar joy and solace.

Do you?
Where is it?

If not, go and find it.
Do not quit
until you have;
it will make all the difference
in/for you.

Kate Leboff has her BA in English/Creative Writing and a Masters in Professional Studies in Publishing. She currently resides in upstate NY with her two adopted pitties. She works in the editorial/production department at a university press full-time and freelance edits other authors' novels. This is her first publication, and she is working on a follow-up collection of poems, a crime/thriller novel, a YA fantasy novel, and a book that is equal parts self-help and humorous self-deprecation.

www.ingramcontent.com/pod-product-compliance
Lightning Source LLC
Chambersburg PA
CBHW040257170426
43192CB00020B/2834